The Essential Tom Marshall

The Essential Tom Marshall

selected by David Helwig
and Michael Ondaatje

The Porcupine's Quill

Library and Archives Canada Cataloguing in Publication

Marshall, Tom, 1938–1993
[Poems. Selections]
The essential Tom Marshall / selected by David Helwig and Michael Ondaatje.

(Essential poets ; 9)
Includes bibliographical references.
ISBN 978-0-88984-353-0

I. Helwig, David, 1938– II. Ondaatje, Michael, 1943– III. Title. IV. Poems. Selections. V. Series: Essential poets (Erin, Ont.) ; 9

PS8576.A758E87 2012 C811'.54 C2012-902602-6

1 2 3 • 14 13 12

Published by The Porcupine's Quill, 68 Main Street, PO Box 160, Erin, Ontario N0B 1T0. http://porcupinesquill.ca

Represented in Canada by the Literary Press Group.
Trade orders are available from University of Toronto Press.

We acknowledge the support of the Ontario Arts Council and the Canada Council for the Arts for our publishing program. The financial support of the Government of Canada through the Canada Book Fund is also gratefully acknowledged.

Canada
Ontario
Ontario Media Development Corporation
Canada Council for the Arts
Conseil des Arts du Canada
ONTARIO ARTS COUNCIL
CONSEIL DES ARTS DE L'ONTARIO

Table of Contents

Foreword

The city of Kingston stood at the centre of Tom Marshall's personal and imaginative universe. He moved to Kingston to study at Queen's university in 1957. In 1993 he died there, in the small brick house he had bought some years before. Though he spent time travelling in Europe after his graduation and later settled in London for a year to work toward a PhD, with a sabbatical year spent in Toronto a few years later, he always returned to the city where his parents had met. For years he lived close to the lake among the fine stone houses built in the nineteenth century when Kingston was in line to become the capital of Canada. In the sixties he inhabited an apartment overlooking the park named for Sir John A. Macdonald and containing a statue of the man. Tom's first long poem was about Macdonald and his park. 'Overlooking the park,' he says in an introduction to the poem, 'I came to feel that there was a thing in it, a vision or Beast, to be observed and recorded.'

Later he wrote a lengthy set of poems, a kind of modernized sonnet cycle, which opens with a dedication to the city of Kingston. *Marine city of my dreams,* he calls it. Anyone who knew Tom in those days can easily trace on the map of memory a stroll down to the lakeshore with its view of Wolfe Island, the trudge to Queen's past the old courthouse, the few blocks to the downtown, the walk back to the apartment on West Street, or in later years to the Annandale Annex, where his windows on one side looked out over tall willows, on the other over a parking lot and the elegant old houses of William Street. Anyone reading his early poems will learn the details of his daily life, as he passed through that rackety, half-gentrified core of the limestone city searching out the mystic fire at the edge of things.

Sight burns us free of love
to green paraphrase
that burns us finally free of sight.

What is probably the earliest poem in this collection, 'Astrology', already suggests some of the qualities of voice and manner that lie at the core of Tom Marshall's poetry. The offhand opening statement – *It's an approach. Say what you like / about it. It's an approach* – leads on to a slyly ironic assertion – *I care more about this / arrangement of words than about you* – and finally the poem that began in a denial of sentiment ends with a high romantic demand – *give me the whole fire of your heart*. A conclusion imposed by a self-dramatizing young poet perhaps, but the calm irony of the opening lines is characteristic, and the poem suggests his range of tones, the balance of humour and seriousness, the way his poems remain lyrical even when he is writing of bitter love, self-abasement, *brilliant restless nights*. In the early park poems the calm insistence of a quiet inward voice urges the reader on to another thought, another stanza.

In this short selection there has not been room to include any of Tom Marshall's ambitious long poems, 'Macdonald Park', 'Islands', 'Cosmic Photographs', 'Fugue for Lonny'. One of the longer poems included here is 'The Lamb', an evocative and powerful elegy dedicated to Susan Alliston; it becomes an invocation of a whole era of artists in London. Some of Tom's poems about London in *The Silences of Fire* suggest that the city could still embody itself – as it did when T.S. Eliot published *The Waste Land* – as a kind of hell. 'The Lamb' plays with that metaphor.

> *The Lamb. Underworld saloon*
> *where Dickens, Wilde and Dylan Thomas drank,*
> *those haunted dilettantes, the poets*
>
> *of Hades and Bloomsbury ... Oh Sue*
> *where are you? You*
> *should be the hostess of this Underworld.*

(In 2010, it came to light that Susan Alliston, to whom 'The Lamb' is dedicated, was the woman with Ted Hughes on the winter night in 1963 when his wife Sylvia Plath committed suicide.)

One of five brothers born into a middle-class family, Tom Marshall was both secretive and obsessive about his personal life. As an undergraduate, he chose history as his main field of study, and he had a consuming sense of the drama of the Canadian past, which played itself out in his poems. He delighted in the fact that John Montgomery, the owner of the tavern where one of the half-comic confrontations of the 1837 rebellion took place, was one of his ancestors. At the time of his death he was completing revisions on a novel on the subject.

In 1980 Tom Marshall's first four books, each named for one of the elements, were brought together in a substantial selection called *The Elements*. In the following years a good deal of his creative energy was taken up by the writing of fiction.

Tom Marshall's final collection of poetry was assembled from material found in his files after his death, some of it highly personal and more direct than the earlier poems, and it included poems that he had kept on hand but not published. The old age and death of his parents was a source for some of his best late poems. 'Dream Sequence', 'The Mother', and 'Words for HSKM' are attempts to come to terms with his strong and ambiguous feelings about his parents, his mother in particular. 'The Mother', a vigorous portrait etched in wormwood, was written and set aside while his mother was still alive; it is impelled by bitterness and anger and yet perhaps contains something that is their exact opposite. 'For HSKM' is an elegy and tries to reach some kind of accommodation.

> *Human mysteries persist, deepen.*
> *There is no resolution. Only pain*
> *familiar and defining, strengthening.*

It has been argued that Tom was not at his best with endings, that sometimes poems are forced to a neat conclusion. Perhaps that's why the last poems are so strong; they open out, don't give in to something; they have a lovely tentativeness. It may be that their new directions in tone and shape are the result of the fact that they were 'unpublishable' poems and for that reason he allowed them a different aesthetic logic.

Tom Marshall's premature death at fifty-five in the small brick house on Victoria Street – where he imagined ghosts and lined up the sayings from Chinese fortune-cookies on his coffee table like some kind of Tarot – left his fine poetry to the merciless inattention of passing time. He is not on hand to help broadcast news of his work, though he is well remembered in Kingston as a figure central to the literary world there for more than two decades.

Everyone likes to believe that the best of poetry will endure, but it doesn't do so without help. Perhaps this collection, assembled by two old friends as a small act of affection and loyalty, will help to bring Tom back as a living voice.

What we did not know
fades with what we did

The park is more like a wood

Dream

The park is more like a wood.
The great trees stand apart
at a respectful distance.

On the night we walk
into the park, lightning falls
and fails, a sensuality turned inward.

Overhead, in waves, the lost fringes
of forest blow, break
under the ghostly stars, and the

early moon bends, beckoning
our lips and bodies back. At this point,
always, I turn and speak to you.

From Here

Beyond the park is the lake.
I cannot see it
from my balcony.

But I see today
a child in the park
running the hard ground
under the red sky, and I

am taken suddenly back
to the favourite photograph,

memory of a memory,
me, leaning, grinning round
the corner of the great tree
laughing the invisible lake,

and I can take that child
as a dwarf of me,
even from here I can see
all the elements are there
heart can find, mind can be –
fire, earth, water, air,
the child in the wood
who laughed around the tree.

Summer

Sun blooms in our bodies
like a soft death,
a warmth that is far
more permanent than love.

We imagine that sun
becomes part of us.
Fools not to know
we must fall into it.

For now the park
opens within, living trees
unlock their secrets
to the whole silence of fire.

And do not ask to love me
but love through me
as now through the ripe tree
the bruise of life burns outward.

Fall

Not only children inherit the park
now the park is a yellow stillness
but old men, perverts of several kinds,
grotesque women with floppy hats and sunglasses –
sitting on benches among their squirrels,
day after day feeding on leaves and paper.

Alone, I watch them from my balcony
as from a dark doorway. I know
they have gone under the hanging leaves
to give themselves to the park.
They would like to sink into the earth
to nourish a tree.

I watch. And I think I see.
Into delicious depths of self-abasement
they are falling. Offering at last
to the unmoved autumnal corridors
the bitter love of the unbeautiful.
So that the world opens, flows.
The park grows wider than light.

For those
who court the earth court not obscenity
but use. O love's too pitiful a word
to comprehend the kindness of the place
that offers them such death –
death eternal, the passion of the earth
trembling at the root of their design.

Day by day they come. And I watch
from the balcony.

(O see
beyond the trees that tower up to heaven
the burning man fall outward into ardent space)

Autobiographies

I

I ate the mint-leaves among the railway cinders.
The sun flamed, at night the trains rumbled, the water-
fall roared: the town splayed upon the terrible fountain.
On the air floats Ponce de Leon's gaudy illusion:
the fast cars, the fast girls who opened their legs,
drunk over the river, roaring in Buffalo,
stumbling over beer-cans on the midnight beaches.
In dreams I slid into the crashing waters
so easily, so easily I thought all waters
lived in my veins and flowed in living fountains.
The blackshirt hoods lounged sulkily on Centre St.,
dark guardians of human pain, warning angels
with truths too simple for the roaring boys.
The mirror of Narcissus lay hid in the wood
a dark enamelled pool flecked with angry stars.

II

The groundhogs nuzzling at the window-panes
in the brilliant moonlight have awakened me
from superb dreams of holocaust and retribution.
These brilliant, restless nights, the torments of hay-fever
exacerbate the itch in the shocked brain.
A woman sleeps, or does not sleep, in another room.
Her white hair electric, outspread, fills the moonlit windows,
she lies against the night and the angry stars
of ten, perhaps twenty years. An owl's cry
is all but lost in the reckless barrage of moonlight,
the loud torrent that breaks and conquers the grotesque shapes
of groundhogs, trees, badgers or whatever wakes.
The wood is lunatic, shaken with incandescent life.
In this house of illness, guilt and moonlight
I am pierced by the white, corrosive eye of God.

Astrology

It's an approach. Say what you like
about it. It's an approach.
Speak of the transience of philosophies;
all are decommissioned at last.
I admit this. It's entirely the point.

I care more about this
arrangement of words than about you.
To return one needs an approach,
'a way of happening',
and any approach will do
in a sense. The one that works
is true (of course, all are true).

Why not then take the intricate
fire of stars as way? Interlocking roses
of our summer day
are no less blasted in the tides of dust.
Why not take penmanship, ornithology?
Why not take you and me?

Can you give me of your
bare instincts enough? Save me
(though the cost may be beyond your ken) ?
Do it then. For I know. But
I must know the full horoscope
of your desire. So give me
conjunctions of dust; make again
the knotted turning of the seasons start;
give me the whole fire of your heart.

Speedboat

The machine, many poets
to the contrary, is not
the enemy.

In our just becoming
world, we wish
on motors as on stars.
All the same. All the best
hopes are for motion.

Spray. Wind. Space.
Reclaimed, a way home.
Disintegrating in gladness,
stung into sweetest pain,
we are racing.

We are racing
to the lost islands
of apples and birds,
islands of wild apples
breaking in flame
behind the eye,

islands of trees
where the nested gulls
alarmed, rise to cry, o cry
the heart's wisdom down
in whirling explosions
that meet and dwindle
our brokenwinged myth.

For everything we do
is the attempt, blind,
speedblown, to unlock
that fire, that fevering
atom's flight that makes
forever back
the winged trajectory,
the strenuous and timeless track.

Derangement

Islands are green mandalas
that turn upon their light.
Bright nerve-tips of wave
curve into air like the faces
of Rilke's rapt angels.

Out in the bays that heave
the afternoon moon's phases
sailboats are elliptical triangles.
Angles of innocent air make delight
of troubled swallows' carving.

Very slowly now we are leaving
our senses in hallowed night.
Sight burns us free of love
to green paraphrase
that burns us finally free of sight.

Notes from a London Diary

I

Specimen Scholar

Morning
on Southampton Row. I gasp
like a fish
drowning in air. A pale

disc of flame
tints the day
poisonous yellow.

Crushed
in the coloured slide
I flounder

to the fetid
B.M.

crouch behind
sooted walls like
one of the antiquities.

II

Nov. 23, 1966

To be left
alone where
there is no vision,

Drunk, strange, alone.
How pathetically
I reach
for the one person
I have met
that I seem to belong to.

III

Nov. 29, 1966

The strange
daytime twilight –

This grey twilight
at three o'clock –

I come home
drunk.

This thing
floods the room
with a mysterious radiance.

I cannot bear
to turn on the lights.

IV

London Nocturne

My nerves are shot.
The sky is bruised blue.
A moon like a torn nail.
Hundreds of city things float
across my sight.
Hundreds of insects.
I hate them all
indiscriminately.

Words in Exile

I

As the year
moves to its darkness, I move
walk, run, cross Russell Square
in the fugitive sunlight. Pigeons,
leaves are flying. Red hydrangeas
burn on the air. Glowing
coals of solstice. How your cheeks grew
hollow with dark
two years ago.

II

LONDON,
the great Beast. Paper
crackles in the Thames, no sky, only white
Presence in the air. I walk
run, cross Russell Square
in the fugitive sunlight.
Think: Agincourt, the burgeoning earth inhabited
by many dead.

III

When my grand-
mother, ELLEN, was buried, not there
but at Niagara, the wind twisted the earth, stung
on the false face of grief. Leaves
rattled along the earth.

IV

The trees
in England are ghostly, behind the eyes
surpassing the moon. Whose white limbs
are theirs, her comeliness. Whose limbs
are white in a thin
drizzle of rain. Trees
are beautiful, and not dismayed
at mere human grief. They turn
on the air. They dance.

V

MATTHEW, my grand-
father died at 93. He did not dance. And if
he burned it was the cold burning of snow. He did not know
how to dance. And fire fell on him. His bones
burn in the burgeoning earth of Agincourt.

VI

And I
shivered that day, in sunlight, fugitive, I
whirling, a leaf caught, and carried to darkness, space, falling
outward from earth, from air, a black
desolate astronaut.

VII

Paper
crackles in the flames, no sky, only white
Presence in the air. Still the rain
holds off, and the humid square
smells like a lover's body. You
are living still. As the year.

VIII

Trees
are beautiful, and not dismayed. Pigeons,
leaves are flying. Red hydrangeas
burn on the air. I move
walk, run. In the white
Presence of the air. The humid square
smells like a lover's body. You
are living still
like a solstice coal.

Interior Monologue #666

'Hydrocephalics are holy, too,
they have
a certain
bloated beatitude ...'

I think I am becoming
a tree. At any rate
something slow, lethargic,
vegetable. I am said
to resemble a rutabaga.

Do rutabagas have leaves
I wonder? I should like
to have leaves at least.
Slow ones. Leaves of pain
perhaps. Leaves of sleep.

It is said the gods
descend at last. In UFO's
perhaps. In BVD's for all
I care. Who cares if gods
descend? They are leaves

of sky, my leaves. Mine,
perhaps yours, I would be generous.
Every day the sky has leaves.
The sky-tree has grey leaves.
The sky-tree is ours.

Coda: Macdonald Park

the park is eternal but I
fall beyond it in the fabulous
whole and silent angel of fire
flying the wound that sings

looking out my window I see
park and lake, leaf and lost desire
curved as music or the universe
to the old eye, the androgynous wings

that move, and moving make
an end of echoes, a virtue
of shifting perspectives, a thing
finally complete, and whole, and moving

Politics

I

They will win, I thought once,
because they have a myth,
The myth shapes their hunger.
And shapes also the faceless
beast made of many longings
who now coalesces in all of us
and surfaces crying 'Liberty!'

He is not good or evil. He is there, simply,
under the snow, under the white eye
of the dream continent
into which we sink further and further
an ancient pain grown ever more urgent
because we thought we left it behind
in Africa, Asia and Europe.

II

An almost monochrome snowscape
is the beginning of our myth.
Against it I have set
the brown and gold richness
of a room, a large room
with three large windows. Snow
flickers like cinema in all of them.

Hypnotic snow. Eradicating time
and banishing history from consciousness
you deceive us and begin us.
How shall we live with such blankness?
Shall we invoke the unjust past
or the equally false Utopian future?
Blood flows: a film over our eyes.

III

Riel, Mackenzie. My own ancestor,
Montgomery, declared to the judge
who sentenced him to hang: 'You think
you can send me to the gallows,
but I tell you that when
you're all frizzling with the devil,
I'll be keeping tavern on Yonge Street!'

He did too. First he was pardoned
and banished to British slave camps
in Van Diemen's Land. Then he dug through a wall
of Kingston's Fort Henry despite
his fractured leg, escaped half-starved to the States
next week, and was finally pardoned
to keep a mean tavern on Yonge Street.

IV

That was the rough trade of our lives:
Riel hanged, Pierre Laporte strangled
in his own chain. History has many
unpleasant surprises for those
who placed her under a glass case labelled
conquest, cross, mosaic-piece, piece
of the peaceable future kingdom.

For now the dreamer wakes,
now the sleeper wakens into time,
and no mythology finally will matter
(theirs or ours) unless it is true
to a single room with its large windows
a single room made of many windows
opening and closing their eyes of cold snow.

from Islands

for the city of Kingston

Marine city of my dreams where it is always
summer.

These islands have awaited us.

                                                            Serene
In the brilliant winter they have known
our absence was a kind of joy.

                                                  They
have gathered our anticipations until
in rich May, in the high summer
we return to them across the waters.

(Sailors, spectre-ships on the lake.

                                                            Sea
and light contracting our repose
to this still hour of white noon.)

                                                  Still, words
between the dead and the living
are difficult.

                              The waters glittering
and sceptical of hopes may answer us:
anticipation is a *kind* of joy.

Strictly Personal

Twilight on snow.
The blue air descends.

If I could
always have been so
open how different
things might have been.

Now I dream
of an endless summer
the lover and the garden
that were always there.

You must live by the dream
however strange the dream.

The Return

It is good to be back
in Canada where things
are so intensely themselves.

The grass, the colour of the
shadow of the grass.
September light separates things

carefully. Trees, clouds, blades
of grass are bathed
in it, cleansed. Waves lift

and ripen in the crackling
air. The brown
pools untouched by wind

in the hollows of large
protruding roots shine
secretly in the park.

Qualifications

(ills that flesh is heir to: mumps
in childhood, bloated grey face, the

child's right eyelid slit through
with barbed wire, later

peritonitis, three black
rubber tubes stuck in, stink

like rotting intestines made external,
piss by catheter, sticky

putrid flow of gut corruption

Other Qualifications

(flat feet, the odd sprained ankle, recurrent flu
running nose, a share of sexual failure

loneliness, boorishness, malice
melancholia, alcoholic shakes

at times, inexplicable black fatigue
of soul, absence of feeling or caring

for days, months of vacancy, nobody home
at the shit-and-blood machine, last seen

asleep, functioning, nobody home but me

Legend

birds screaming in garden wind rising

eyes closed in meditation I hear it acutely

leaves moving squirrels birds foraging

a nervous fury of eating eating,

till all garden is intoxicating fruit

wind a dinosaur or huge snake

devouring mortal tainted paradise as

lovers feast on one another's jellied eyes

Second Legend

the trouble is there is no
sorcerer but only apprentices
man is the political animal
who knows paranoia is power
demons rise up, atoms split
there is so much incomplete magic
inchoate worlds and spells
in the wind of power

the apprentice broods in his room
but one day he will begin
a strange and dangerous journey
through the transformed garden
where wind and mantis-tree
earth and singing air wait for him

The Friends

It is always night, he is silent.

Outside, great spaces
between trees and stars.

Cold spaces of summer night.

Under the woman's lively words
the emptiness, the spaces.

He is mostly silent.

The books are banked
against the cold stars.

The children are asleep, the
clatter of guests
evaporates on black air.

Everything is falling away.

Words, the words recede.

Where are they?

Even the house, even the flesh recedes.

He is mostly silent.

There is a room, windows, trees.

It is always night.

The Lamb

for Susan Alliston

It is her absence makes the place haunted....
More desolate than a tube's
escalator at night, moving rows
of empty steps, receding perspective....

Above the din I hear her debutante voice
throaty and sociable. I cannot
ever think of her as dead, I
wonder if I am not the one dead

and this the underground, these
glass panels, bright bottles and glass-cased photos
of old actresses. The sun bends
through glazed panes into an undersea.

Saturday afternoons under water
swamped with gossip and bitter
we talked the dark age away.
Everything's different now, it seems a much

older crowd. A duller, sadder crowd.
I want to see her striding suddenly
darkhaired and gap-toothed, greeting everyone,
a wide smile, a wool dress with dangling chains.

Her front was too strong for her pain
ever to be too obvious. (A year later the last
days, unconscious with her large eyes
open, staring. The last thing,

the last *coherent* thing
she said to me: 'Tom,
I'm sorry. You came back
and I'm useless like this, I feel

as if I'm on my *death*-bed'
or words to that effect, I
didn't write them down. She
apologized for lapsing into sleep

helplessly. She offered lemonade
to visitors.... The Lamb. Underworld saloon
where Dickens, Wilde and Dylan Thomas drank,
those haunted dilettantes, the poets

of Hades and Bloomsbury.... Oh Sue,
where are you? You
should be the hostess of this Underworld.
God knows, you were too kind and too

self-sacrificing to live in the other one.
You suppressed your Arian fire
yet lived recklessly knowing
you would die sooner rather than late.

(Your body was destroyed with fire:
ashes that drift on a wind of dream
better than the dull thud of earth
on a rainy hill here or in Africa....

I think now that you were right.
Expending yourself, shortening your time
to live more intensely, more generously.
You were not gentle with the English night....

They're throwing us out now, it's overcast
in Lamb's Conduit Street.... Ash on the air
of London.... Ash over Russell Square....
I walk to the tube as quickly as I can.

Approaching 38

I travelled space-time to a place
where my father was young

I saw people walking in cities

A sensitive boy, good-natured,
easy to work with   Well-liked

His remoteness not obvious then

I see him chatting
shyly, cheerfully
with girls in the warehouse

There is blessing on youth, I
place it there

Christmas Travel Poems

i

A kind of howling wind in the walls
a faint sound on the inner ear
accompanies the family Christmas
in the high-rise apartment.

It is only the air-vents
in the two bathrooms
but it seems to me
that it was always there
in every house
we ever lived in.

ii

In the dream I am
flying though not alone
in a gold storm of leaves,
there is a great
singing over the field
the trees the stone buildings
a company in flight …

I am protected
by many unknown companions.

iii

As the train moved into the blizzard
the children began counting the snowflakes.
'How long,' said the unknown lady,
'will it take to count them all?'

from Summer of '77

July 1, 1977

The Atlantic beats against the rocks at
Peggy's Cove continually. The huge
textured rocks! Bold stones! Great speckled eggs or
bones of female earth! Glooskap's daughter born
of crash and shock, foam rising in the air
a perpetual fountain. Crash and shock!

We clamber over boulders. We are small
animals at tidal pools. And the eye
moves outward irresistibly in salt
undertow. Moves into teeming death, that
ocean overwhelms all differences,
all pride surrenders to that salty pull
and heave, crash and shock of great Atlantic
waves beating perpetually on rock.

Field Syllabics

for Dennis Lee

September: paradise
receding. Lakewaves gleam
at the end of the street.
Clarity returns to
the city, the islands.
The islands on the air.

Shimmering, glancing gold
on water, the sun binds
us to the earth whose bounds
are built and bent by us,
bewildered as we are,
burdened as we may be.

A field of flowing grass,
blowing grass: Wolfe Island.
A bright white stone farmhouse.
A field-flow forever:
mind-field of particles,
field of force in the world.

Distant leaves move gently,
still green against pale blue.
Their movement is the mind's
or the marked molecules'
movement under mind's moves:
a mind-field undermined?

September: paradise
receding. Lakewaves gleam,
distant leaves move gently,
still green against pale blue.
A field of flowing grass,
blowing grass: Wolfe Island.

The city, the islands.
The islands on the air.
Bewildered as we are,
burdened as we may be.
Mind-field of particles.
Field of force in the world.

Dream Sequence: 17 May 1984

The prologue is a party, a room
where several friends of mine, seated,
converse. Two older women, handsome
in different ways, are also there.
One is formidable, English, not unkind.

Then it was a subway platform with
many women, men. I found myself
in flight where others trudged
through tunnels from station to station.
It was underground, uterine, female.

I am flying down Davenport Road
on the back of a dark-haired lady.
From behind she looks like Doris Lessing.
In front she is a sharp-beaked bird.

We rose beautiful, glorious up over the city

where giant serpents writhed in the streets below.
I floated off the she-bird's back holding
onto her harpy's wing for a last moment drifting

to look my last on her cruel beak and claws
and see they are no longer dangerous

to me. Then I let go and flew
glorious by myself: I am standing

in a public building with friends
and colleagues of both sexes when
I note my dead father waiting

quiet by the door. Young, smiling there.
We go outside to talk. He asks
if I still live partly in that place. I say

yes: my picture is there. He says
he wants to attend on me.

As he left, fading or disintegrating
in a kind of atomic ash, reddish,
I asked: how is it where you are?
He replied, old, facetious, that there wasn't
much *physical leave*. There's no place

perfect, I said, still soaring.
He was gone then, smiling. And I

returned now to my people, my life, my
dream-interpretations that offer both

a friend's sustaining love, a woman's death.

Daedalus, Icarus

1

Saturday: rain, and wind howling,
harrowing of hell. Sunday

he is rising, calm
from earth's tomb into
blue emptinesses of sky.
A silver bird
takes him north and north.

Here earth's abandoned things sprawl,
float in sunshine.
Cats white and black
nose out their territories
over brown grass, occasional
green shoots. Here

branches wave in air, other branches lie
broken in April sun
where squirrels dart
and small birds alight
on porches and power lines.

I go about my tasks. Uncrucified.
A silver cross takes you north and north.

2

You fell. And fell.
Over. My fear of you
falling. Come true.
The police, the ambulance.
You lying on the drenched
earth, the gravel,

your face not even
broken. 'He fell off
the roof.'
          You were flirting
with it. My fear for you
falling.

3

          A maze of
rainlight. Glamorous. August. I
watched over you.

Grasping my hand. Tight.

Sedated, but frequently
smiling. At dawn
warm drizzle persists.
Misty lake outside window.

A humid, dopey day. Uninjured,
a miracle except for that
slightly fractured shoulder
you fell on,
but too weak
to walk without listing.
You doze a lot.

(Dreaming of flight?)

4

I wondered, of course,
how much I stimulated you.

My own flights are tempered now.
I survived my fall, my youth.

I survived my thirty-third birthday,
that fell on Good Friday.

5

A silver bird takes you north. Safe.

And I am with you now, here
in sun-borne flight

since that rainy night's amaze.

'We are dying, we are dying, we are all of us dying'

– D.H. Lawrence, 'The Ship of Death'

Even the red rocks look like animals
in Africa. We have been travelling
through a huge, dusty antechamber
to that room we all come to.
We have our moment, then become the past,
join with rock and earth and whirling dust
and all its metamorphoses to be.

Yet something more emanates from this.
Like all bright creatures vanishing in love
we leave our magic images behind us.
Let us persist, then, with what we yet have.
In our long, bewildered dying, let us live.

Written in the pleasant garden of the New Arusha Hotel,
at the north-south centre of Africa,
while waiting for lunch, 23 August 1989.

Flight

alone in a cold waste of light
the final skater   a disappearing speck
in a flashing   gold jacket
still carves himself a place

while the sun falls
against the bland sky   brushes
islands   trees   low-leaning clouds
aside with such grace

the landscape itself bends
focuses its bright eye
upon this one

gleaming human response   the far
gold poetry of lonely flight
into the golden sun

To Whom It May Concern

This book-panelled room is moving
at a great speed throughout the universe
(and this is the kind of statement
my panelled reviewers loathe).
I am not on any drug, even alcohol.
I am not hallucinating. (I suspect I am incapable of it.)
Everything is exactly as it is.
And this panelled room is moving
at a great speed throughout the universe.

Wave-Movements

1

grapeleaves, black currants, tiger-lilies (tall!)
raspberries and yellow roses riding
winds of three summers in the back garden,

a wave-movement that includes me at last
motionless as a moving ship that glides
only on resonant July silence

(I saw last year the god of the garden,
a face only, Greekish, in foliage:
drinking wine all afternoon helped me see),

a leaf-movement that alters the blue sky
now become so strangely like green water
or green fire that burns and unmakes all things

into strange movements and bright frequencies
in summer garden on the turning earth
of successive dreamlike July daytimes,

2

a glory of September gale, whitecaps
rising, trees agitated, branches break-
ing in the wild gold sunlight that flickers

on high green leaves, lake and wind informing
a whole city: the last day of my good
father's seventy-four years of living

though I did not know that then as I walked
against strong rushing air to look at the
waves, the waves and whitecaps surging shoreward

Commit the flowers to the flames
that flow over him.
Consign the ashes to the air.
All gold-blown days dim

Into evening and afterglow.
What we did not know
fades with what we did.
Those flowers burning on the coffinlid.

yellow roses even in September
in the back garden of my brother's house
on this day of my father's funeral,

a sunlit garden on the turning earth
of successive dreamlike lives and movements
of leaves and men, and now pungent grapesmell

filling my nostrils in this autumn warmth,
this richness of leaf-galaxies, lilies
and spent bushes: raspberries, currants gone.

The Mother

1

A dwindled heap
of raw nerves, arthritic hip.
Her weakness takes the edge
off his bitter love.
Compassion becomes possible.

But there is no pity
for the dwindled witch
in her abandoned quarry
(gouged out of high hill
that might have been vision).

She hid herself in this closed space.
She wounded him
with her possessive fears,
gardens, carefully hidden house.
Sweet Elysium in the flagstone cracks.

2

In spring, floating clouds
of gold forsythia.
Too beautiful, nauseous.
She cultivates the brief, dusty roses.
Her children are afraid of her.

The nervous girl, escaped
to college, read Rupert Brooke.
Her father, granite man,
walks in the garden
though she walled him out.

She mouths her pieties
but she hates God
with splendid, unrecognized ferocity.
Her soft lies are misted forsythia
she cannot see through.

3

But then, alone, she cries,
She is as fierce as crumbling roses.
She moves on the edge of hill
feeling the full wind
sharply in her bones.

So much life, so little charity
cannot admit its burning.
The fall sumacs flame at her.
There is no pity
for the dwindled witch.

(Her second son broods
on these injustices.
He looks to the blind duck
in the bathtub, to the lilac-tree.
His wagon is called Champion.)

Words For HSKM (1910–1991)

The Kennedy profile recumbent
is like a craggy mountain range
rising above the oak casket.

Time's scythe has had its way with her.
The Ancient of Days has drawn a line
around her. She survives herself no more.

For years she had been receding
little by little. She had been
remembered in dreams as younger, stronger.

A shrunken woman, kindly, distant,
not that terrifying sorceress
not yet the strong, protective matrona.

Mother, in your darkness and light
I grew. Your love of music and reading.
Your hatred of space and freedom.

Curious contradictions of
anxiety, nerves, depression
persisting through generations

of Kennedys working the land.
Whence comes all that depth of darkness?
From Scotland's internecine turmoil?

Human mysteries persist, deepen.
There is no resolution. Only pain
familiar and defining, strengthening.

from Voyages

To sleep with you
is like so many voyages
to places I wasn't sure existed
before. No tears, no claims
or jealousies intrude
upon the wise flesh
a lover both impersonal
and real. I want now
to make love to each one
of your individual
freckles.

No Way

There is no help for it, and no way out.

In my dream I move into a further room
only to find your ghostly face accuses me of love.
We can sometimes be too strong for our own good.
I realize now that I have never known you
except partially, dimly, as though you moved
really in shadows, in the hollows

of the dark face that so delighted me.

Sonnets of Scorpio

You told me he stood at the window
and wept the ending of his innocence
outlined on the lamplit world
the rain falling soundless before him
and would not turn until you turned away
and would not speak
                                        and I
would rather you forgot that day
that singular budding of pain
in the rich may
                                        and I
would come to you clear-hearted
serene in the brilliant winter
the dark shape that wept at the window

(   )

I suppose I could place you

in the prism, parentheses
(eyes the colour of rain, hair like misted forsythia

etc.) break you down
into parts (poems), into a cold or a cool

pastoral or two, make you
immortal (in a manner of speaking)

fix you in some line formulation
(e.g., eyes: rain; hair: misted forsythia)

except, except you wriggle better in reality
than in that artifice to which

I'd gather you (as priggish poets did Persephone)
and god knows you're still a pretty fair piece

so I think I'll hold on a while,
making like a good lover,

and make no lovely (   ) today.

About the Author

Tom was born in Niagara Falls, Ontario, April 9, 1938, the second of five sons of Douglas Woodworth Marshall and Helen Steele Kennedy Marshall. His mother's ancestors were Loyalists who were granted large tracts of land in the Agincourt area of Ontario, and the Kennedy name endures on various roads and public buildings in the area. His father's family emigrated from Scotland in the 1840s. Tom's parents met at Queen's University. His maternal grandfather had also attended the university, graduating in 1898.

Tom grew up mostly in Niagara Falls, though from 1943 to 1945 the family lived in Joplin, Missouri, and Memphis, Tennessee, where his father, a chemical engineer, worked on loan to the British American Powder company, under a special wartime arrangement. Helen Marshall had graduated with a degree in library science, but, according to her son Andrew, she 'never worked in her field except at home, amassing a library of thousands of books'.

After graduating from Niagara Falls Collegiate in 1957, Tom attended Queen's, where he studied history and English. At this period those teaching in the English Department included Malcolm Ross, then Canadian literature's most significant critic and editor, and the poets Douglas LePan and George Whalley. In Tom Marshall's final year he edited the *Queen's Journal*, and after graduation he went to Europe, travelling around the continent on a motorbike with a friend from his undergraduate years, David Glassco.

In 1963 he returned to Queen's and began a master's degree, writing his thesis on the poetry of A.M. Klein. A few years later he would edit a book of essays on Klein's poetry. He was involved with the development of the Queen's literary magazine, *Quarry*, into a national literary quarterly, and in 1965 along with two Queen's associates, Colin Norman and Tom Eadie, he published a joint collection called *The Beast with Three Backs*, under the imprint of Quarry Press. He began to teach at Queen's in 1965–66. At this period a number of young writers who were later to publish significant poetry and fiction were associated with the university and with *Quarry* magazine. Among them were Douglas Barbour, Gail Fox, David Helwig, Stuart MacKinnon, and Michael Ondaatje. Tom also became friends with Al Purdy, a connection that endured until his death.

In 1966–67, Tom spent the year in England, where he enrolled at the University of London, pursuing a doctorate, writing a thesis on the poetry of D.H. Lawrence. Though he never completed the degree, his thesis became a substantial critical book, *Psychic Mariner: A Reading of the Poems of D.H. Lawrence,* published in the USA by Viking Press, in England by Heinemann, and in Canada by Macmillan.

In the late sixties and early seventies Tom moved back and forth between Kingston and London. His English literary agent was Olwyn Hughes, and he became acquainted with Ted Hughes and a number of other British poets. He taught each year at Queen's, and he settled in Sydenham Ward, the oldest part of Kingston, first in an apartment in an old house on West Street overlooking Macdonald Park and the courthouse, and later in a dim and rather romantic apartment attached to the Annandale building nearby.

His first collection of poetry, *The Silences of Fire,* was published by Macmillan of Canada in 1969. On the same list, and with a matching cover, was Gwendolyn MacEwen's *The Shadow Maker,* and she and Tom Marshall became friends. Within a year he saw published his Lawrence book and the collection of essays on A.M. Klein. He kept up his relationship with *Quarry* magazine, and became editor, publisher and patron of Quarry Press as it published poetry books by George Bowering, Gail Fox, Stuart MacKinnon, and Len Gasparini.

From 1973 to 1978 Tom was the poetry editor of the *Canadian Forum.* He continued to teach both graduate and undergraduate students of Canadian literature, and in 1979 he published *Harsh and Lovely Land,* the first of two collections of essays on Canadian writing.

In 1978 Tom published a novel, *Rosemary Goal,* which made some use of an earlier, abandoned novel and which was the first of the seven volumes of fiction that appeared in the next years; the most successful of them, *Adele at the End of the Day,* was released and well-reviewed in the USA. His last novel, *The Adventures of John Montgomery,* makes significant use of his family's early history in Ontario.

In 1982 Tom left the Annandale and bought a small house. He continued to write, teach, edit and publish. Over the next years, he travelled to China, Mexico, Norway and Africa. In 1992 he spent several days in hospital after a heart attack, and late one night in April of 1993 he suffered a second and fatal heart attack in his house on Victoria Street.

Tom Marshall: A Bibliography

POETRY:

The Beast With Three Backs (with Tom Eadie and Colin Norman). Kingston: Quarry Press, n.d. (1965).
The Silences of Fire. Toronto: Macmillan, 1969.
Magic Water. Kingston: Quarry Press, 1971.
The Earth Book. Ottawa: Oberon Press, 1974.
The White City. Ottawa: Oberon Press, 1976.
The Elements. Ottawa: Oberon Press, 1980.
Playing with Fire. Ottawa: Oberon Press, 1984.
Dance of the Particles. Kingston: Quarry Press, 1984.
Ghost Safari. Ottawa: Oberon Press, 1991.
Some Impossible Heaven of the Senses. Ottawa: Oberon Press, 1994.

CRITICISM:

The Psychic Mariner: A Reading of the Poems of D.H. Lawrence. London and New York: Heineman and Viking Press, 1970.
A.M. Klein. Edited and with an introduction by Tom Marshall. Toronto: Ryerson Press, 1970.
Harsh and Lovely Land: The Major Canadian Poets and the Making of a Canadian Tradition. Vancouver: University of British Columbia Press, 1979.
Multiple Exposures, Promised Lands: Essays on Canadian Poetry and Fiction. Kingston: Quarry Press, 1992.

FICTION:

Rosemary Goal. Ottawa: Oberon Press, 1978. (Harper Collins, paper.)
Glass Houses. Ottawa: Oberon Press, 1985.
Adele at the End of the Day. Toronto: Macmillan, 1987. (Vintage Books, 1990.)
Voices on the Brink. Toronto: Macmillan, 1988. (Faber and Faber, paper.)
Changelings. Toronto: Macmillan, 1991. (McClelland and Stewart, paper.)
Goddess Disclosing. Kingston: Quarry Press, 1992.
The Adventures of John Montgomery. Kingston: Quarry Press, 1995.